ERIC M. ATTIO

The Viral Outlaws

First published by Eric M. Attio 2026

INQUIRIES

For all rights, licensing, and permissions, please contact:

Eric M. Attio

Vero Beach, FL

www.ericmattio.com

First edition

ISBN: 978-1-969453-04-5

This book was professionally typeset on Reedsy.
Find out more at reedsy.com

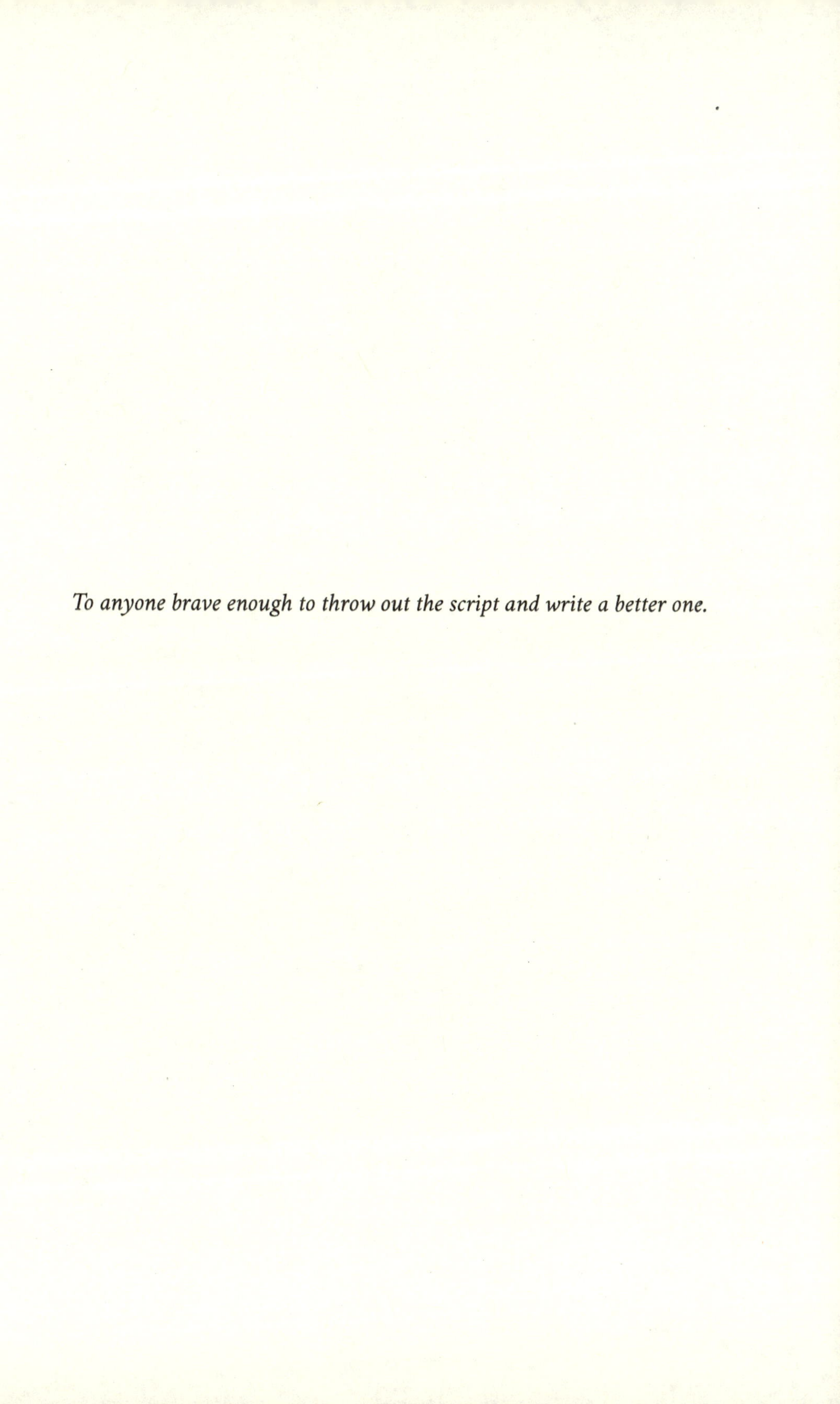

To anyone brave enough to throw out the script and write a better one.

Contents

The Viral Outlaws

A Play in Two Acts
A Comedy

By Eric M. Attio

CHARACTER & CASTING GUIDE

CHARACTER & CASTING GUIDE

CASTING OVERVIEW

Minimum Cast: 5 actors (2 on-stage leads, 1 supporting, 2 voice actors doubling roles)

Ideal Cast: 7-8 actors (2 leads, 1 supporting, 5 individual voice actors)

Set: Single prison cell. Bars stage left. Two bunks.

ON-STAGE CHARACTERS

KEVIN RICHARDSON (Lead)

Age: Mid-30s

Gender: Male

The Role:

Kevin is the engine of Act One. He crashed a live televised awards show and performed seven minutes of unscripted comedy to forty million people. In prison, he is a legend. On stage, he needs to be magnetic enough that the audience believes strangers would stop what they were doing to listen to him. He uses humor as both weapon and shield. He is relentlessly optimistic because the alternative terrifies him.

What to Look For:

This actor needs to be genuinely funny. Not just skilled at delivering written jokes, but someone with natural comedic instinct. Kevin improvises, riffs, and adjusts his energy to his audience. The actor should have the ability to hold a room with a monologue and the charisma to command attention from the moment he speaks. Think stand-up energy filtered through real intelligence.

Underneath the humor is deep pain: abandonment by his father, a failed acting career, the fear that he is nothing without an audience. The magic of this role is the pivot. One moment he's getting the biggest laugh in the room. The next moment, the armor drops and we see the wound. The actor who can do both in a single beat is the right Kevin. If Kevin is only funny, the play becomes a sitcom. If he is funny and wounded, it becomes a story about survival.

Key Audition Moments:

The awards show monologue in Act One Scene 1 (comedic command and storytelling). The fight in Act One Scene 3 (emotional range, from sharp cruelty to raw honesty in two pages). The 3 AM confession in Act Two Scene 2 (can he be still, quiet, and lost when the performance stops working?).

Physical Notes:

Average build. Unremarkable appearance is actually part of the character. His power comes entirely from voice, timing, and mind. Someone who looks like you would pass them on the street without noticing, until they opened their mouth.

Voice:

Quick and sharp, capable of rapid-fire delivery and also capable of real silence. Needs to fill a theater during monologues and drop to a whisper for the late-night scenes. Range matters more than volume.

ROB WILSON (Lead)

Age: Mid-30s

Gender: Male

The Role:

Rob has the biggest arc in the play. He enters as a man who wants to disappear, humiliated and shut down, convinced his life is over after dropping fake money from a plane as a real estate marketing stunt. He exits as someone who has chosen uncertainty over safety, purpose over comfort. He resists, retreats, fights, breaks, and builds. Rob is the emotional center of the play even when Kevin is doing all the talking.

What to Look For:

An actor who communicates internal states with minimal dialogue. In Act One, Rob's best acting happens in silence: the moment he almost smiles, the beat where he stops pretending not to listen, the way his body shifts before he says a word. This actor needs extraordinary stillness and the ability to make an audience lean forward during a pause.

Rob's journey moves through shame, anger, grief, hope, fear, and commitment. Each scene requires a different register. He also needs to be genuinely funny during the fight, where his anger brings out sharp wit that surprises everyone including himself. The line 'This cage is the only place you've ever mattered' is a good test: it needs to land as both cruel and true at the same time.

Key Audition Moments:

Act One Scene 2: dismantling Kevin's pitch (holding ground against a dominant personality). Act One Scene 3: the fight, especially the prison line (comedic timing born from anger). Act Two Scene 1: the Bulletproof Glass conviction, from 'She's not going to say no' through 'We can save her career' (passion without performance, belief that surprises himself). Act Two Scene 2: choosing the company over his wife (making an impossible choice feel inevitable). Act Two Scene 3: alone after Kevin leaves, writing the letter (carrying the climax solo).

Physical Notes:

Should feel ordinary. Not imposing. The ill-fitting jumpsuit in Scene 1 should emphasize how out of place he feels. By Act Two, the same actor should seem different, not because anything external changed, but because he changed.

Voice:

Quiet in Act One. Not timid, but controlled. Chooses words carefully, says less than he thinks. When he opens up, it should feel like a dam breaking. By Act Two, more authority, but never Kevin's showmanship. His power is conviction, not performance.

Chemistry Note:

Kevin and Rob work best when they feel like genuine opposites who become genuine partners. By Act Two they are equals with different strengths. Auditioning them together is worth the time. The pairing that listens and responds and surprises each other will serve the play better than two individually strong actors who don't connect.

OFFICER MARTINEZ (Supporting)

Age: Flexible (30s-50s)

Gender: Female (could be rewritten male if needed)

The Role:

Martinez is the audience surrogate, the skeptic who secretly believes. Corrections officer, nine years on Block C. She has seen every kind of inmate and every kind of plan. Her survival mechanism is professional distance. But Kevin and Rob get under her armor.

What to Look For:

An actor who communicates warmth through toughness. Martinez never says anything sentimental, but the audience should feel she is rooting for them. She makes 'Don't make me lose my two hundred dollars' feel like 'I believe in you.' Dry wit is essential, funny without trying to be.

A Note on the Balance:

Martinez lives in the tension between her professional armor and her human investment in these two men. She has chosen that armor for good reasons. The most interesting version of this character lets both sides coexist without resolving the tension. The audience should sense she is a different person outside these walls.

Key Audition Moments:

The speech after the fight in Act One Scene 3 (the most important non-lead speech in the play). The bet reveal in Act Two Scene 2 (meaning inside a joke). 'Wilson. Eight months.' after Kevin's departure in Act Two Scene 3 (everything in two words).

Physical Notes:

Should feel like someone who has spent years on her feet. Comfortable in her body. Moves with efficiency, not grace. Uniform is a second skin, not a costume.

Stage Time:

Six to eight moments, most brief. Each appearance shifts the scene. Every entrance is a change in atmospheric pressure.

OFF-STAGE VOICES

The five voices function as a Greek chorus: unseen inmates in neighboring cells who comment on, challenge, and witness Kevin and Rob's journey. Each has a distinct personality and dramatic function. The play works best when the audience can tell them apart by sound alone. Each voice has its own rhythm, its own worldview, its own reason for listening.

RADAR (Voice - The Heart)

Gender: Male

Age Range: Any

Function:

The emotional reader. He notices what nobody else does: shifts in mood, unspoken pain, the moment someone is pretending to be okay. First to ask 'you alright?' and last to accept a dishonest answer.

What to Look For:

Warmth. Genuine, unforced warmth. His voice should feel like a hand on your shoulder. Not soft, he has been through things, but he has retained his empathy. Think of the friend who doesn't give advice, just asks the right question.

Key Lines:

'New guy's hurting, Kevin' (end of Scene 1, establishes his function in three words). 'He watched the whole video though' (end of Scene 2, finds hope nobody else saw). 'He said it' (end of Act One, quiet witness).

Casting Note:

Radar has the final voice line of Act One Scene 1 and the first emotional check-in after Kevin's departure. He bookends the play's emotional arc. The voice should be distinctive enough that the audience recognizes it instantly.

CLICKS (Voice - The Strategist)

Gender: Male

Age Range: 20s (younger than Kevin and Rob)

Function:

The digital native. Understands virality as a system: algorithms, engagement, conversion, content cycles. Young but sharp. The business consultant they didn't know they needed.

What to Look For:

Sharpness and youthful energy. Talks fast, thinks faster. Enthusiastic without being naive. When he asks about conversion strategy it should sound like someone who has done his homework, not a kid quoting a YouTube video.

Key Lines:

'Who is your first client? You have services, a name, but no portfolio' (the practical challenge). 'Her name is Glass. And she got shattered' (Act Two Scene 1, catches the name that becomes the Bulletproof Glass campaign, his biggest contribution to the play). 'You need a call to action' (after Rob's pitch, real strategist thinking). 'Get the website up within two weeks' (systems thinking during a goodbye).

Casting Note:

Should sound noticeably younger than the other voices. The age difference matters. He represents the generation that grew up understanding attention as currency.

CHALK (Voice - The Pragmatist)

Gender: Male

Age Range: 40s-50s (older than Kevin and Rob)

Function:

The veteran. Eleven years inside. He has watched countless inmates leave with grand plans and watched almost all of them fail. He is the hardest sell on the tier. When he finally expresses belief, it is the most meaningful endorsement in the play.

What to Look For:

Gravitas. Weight. A voice that sounds lived in. He doesn't waste words. Should sound like someone who has seen everything and been impressed by very little. He delivers devastating honesty without malice. Not cruel, just experienced. The actor who understands that difference will find this character.

Key Lines:

'Guy last year had a food truck plan. Know where he is now? Back in here' (establishes his worldview). 'They didn't have what you two have' (first crack, and it should feel enormous). 'You're the first one I'm going to worry about' (full concession, no sentimentality).

Casting Note:

Deepest or most grounded voice on the tier. Identifiable by sound alone. His eventual belief should feel like a tectonic shift, not a gentle warming.

THE SAGE (Voice - The Philosopher)

Gender: Male

Age Range: Any (voice suggests wisdom, not necessarily age)

Function:

Intellectual and spiritual voice. Probably white-collar crime. Speaks in considered, almost poetic language. Speaks rarely, no more than four or five times per act. When he speaks, the play pauses to reflect.

What to Look For:

Rich, measured voice. Never rushes. Each word chosen. Thoughtful without being pretentious. His observations should feel like gifts, not lectures. Think of a professor who speaks once during a seminar and everyone remembers what he said.

Key Lines:

'If people can laugh at their leaders, they cannot revere them' (Act One Scene 1). 'The seed does not announce itself when it takes root' (Act One Scene 2). 'The performer and the mirror' (Act Two Scene 1). 'I had a wife once. She gave me the same choice' (Act Two Scene 2, the only time the Sage speaks from personal experience rather than philosophy). 'The tree does not remember being afraid of the dark' (final scene).

Casting Note:

The Sage's power is his silence. When he speaks, the play pauses to listen. That economy is what makes him the conscience of the play.

THE CRITIC (Voice - The Cynic)

Gender: Male

Age Range: Any

Function:

Voice of doubt, sarcasm, and uncomfortable truth. His armor of contempt is almost, but not quite, impenetrable. He voices the audience's own skepticism. His arc is the subtlest in the play: three small cracks across six scenes revealing a man who wants to believe but is terrified of disappointment.

What to Look For:

Impeccable comic timing with dry, sardonic delivery. He gets some of the biggest laughs in the play. Uses wit as a weapon because sincerity has hurt him before. Sharp edge, but not mean. The audience should enjoy him even when he is being difficult.

The Three Cracks:

These are the moments where the armor slips. FIRST: 'I'm not crying. Shut up' (end of Act One Scene 3, nobody accused him, and the denial is the confession). SECOND: 'That's either the bravest or the stupidest' / '...Fair enough' (Act Two Scene 2, conceding without admitting he is moved). THIRD: 'They might actually pull this off' (last line of the play, whispered, almost involuntary, allowing himself to hope). These three moments are his entire emotional journey. They work best when they're small.

Casting Note:

The Critic has the last line of the play. It needs to give the audience permission to hope. The right actor makes it sound like a prayer.

STAGING OPTIONS FOR VOICES

Option A (Minimal): Completely off-stage with microphones. Voices from darkness. Emphasizes isolation: you hear people but never see them.

Option B (Partial): Microphones at stage edges in dim light. Audience sees figures but not faces. Creates a sense of community.

Option C (Recommended): Silhouettes behind scrims or bars upstage, suggesting neighboring cells. Allows physical reactions: leaning in during the fight, pulling back during quiet moments, without breaking the illusion. The silhouettes become an audience-within-the-audience, mirroring how we watch the play.

DOUBLING GUIDE (5-ACTOR MINIMUM)

Actor 1: KEVIN (on-stage throughout)

Actor 2: ROB (on-stage throughout)

Actor 3: MARTINEZ (on-stage for specific moments)

Actor 4: RADAR + CHALK (differentiate through pitch and pacing: Radar quicker and lighter, Chalk slower and deeper)

Actor 5: CLICKS + THE CRITIC + THE SAGE (widest range required: young and fast, dry and sharp, measured and resonant)

No scene requires all three doubled voices in rapid succession.

A NOTE TO DIRECTORS

This play lives or dies on the relationship between Kevin and Rob. Everything else, the chorus, Martinez, the staging, the set, supports that central bond. If you cast two actors who make each other better on stage, who listen to each other, who surprise each other, the play works.

Auditioning them together is the best investment of time in the casting process. Put them in a room, give them the fight scene from Act One Scene 3, and watch. If they make each other dangerous, if the room changes when they lock in, that's your cast.

Thank you for bringing this play to life. I wrote it believing that the right company would find it. If you're reading this, you might be that company.

RIGHTS & PERMISSIONS

ACT ONE: SCENE ONE

SCENE 1: ROB ARRIVES

Lights up on a prison cell. Two bunks, a metal toilet/sink combo, and bars stage left. Sparse, institutional, and gray. ***KEVIN*** *sits on the lower bunk, animated, gesturing as he tells a story to unseen inmates in neighboring cells. He's mid-thirties, with an average build and an unremarkable appearance: which is exactly his point. He doesn't look like a comedian, but the moment he speaks, you understand he's dangerously smart and funny.*

KEVIN:

...so I'm standing backstage at the Oscars, live, coast to coast, with forty million people watching, wearing a headset I bought at Best Buy and a lanyard I made on Canva for maybe twelve bucks. And there are people everywhere: producers with clipboards, stylists with lint rollers, and publicists whispering into phones like they're coordinating a military operation. And nobody, nobody, looks at me twice. You know why?

RADAR *(offstage)*:

Because you looked like you belonged.

KEVIN:

Because I looked like I belonged! That's the whole trick. You put on a headset and carry a clipboard and walk with purpose, and the entire world just lets you through. The system isn't held together by security; it's held together by the assumption that everyone's playing their part.

THE CRITIC *(offstage, dry)*:

Riveting. Please, continue narrating your crimes to an audience of criminals.

KEVIN:

Thank you, Critic, I will. So I'm backstage, and I can hear the show happening. The host is doing his opening monologue: safe jokes, nothing that would offend anyone, and nothing that would make anyone actually think. And I'm watching it on a monitor, and I'm thinking, "This is supposed to be comedy? This is supposed to be the best we've got?"

CLICKS *(offstage)*:

How'd you get past the stage manager? Those people don't miss anything.

KEVIN:

Good question, Clicks. I walked right up to her, with a clipboard, a headset, and total confidence, and I said, "We've got a presenter change for the next segment. Network notes. They want fresh energy." And she looks at me, and she looks at her sheet, and she goes, "Nobody told me about this." And I said, and this is the key, I said, "Yeah, that's why I'm telling you now. You know how it is with last-minute changes." And she just sighed, like this was the fortieth problem of the night and she didn't have time to fight it. She waved me through.

THE SAGE *(offstage, measured)*:

People rarely question confidence. It costs too much energy.

KEVIN:

Exactly. So now I'm in the wings, stage right. I can see the audience: two thousand people in formal wear, plus forty million at home. And there's this transition moment, with lights shifting and the teleprompter resetting, and I just walked out. No introduction. No permission. Center stage. I took the mic off the stand. And the first thing out of my mouth, as I see this security guard stage left, hand on his taser, looking at me like I'm a bomb threat, I go, "Relax! Relax. Put the taser down, Greg. I saw your name tag when we were chatting by the loading dock. You look like a Greg. Everyone just take a breath."

CHALK *(offstage)*:

Was his name actually Greg?

KEVIN:

No idea. But he looked like a Greg. And the audience laughed because they thought it was part of the show. That's the beautiful part: for the first thirty seconds, nobody knew I wasn't supposed to be there. So I kept going. I said, "First off, I want to thank God for the lack of a locking mechanism on that backstage door. Incredible. I want to thank my critics, specifically the ones who said I'd never get on network TV. Technically, I'm trespassing, but look at the ratings! You're welcome."

CLICKS:

And they're still laughing?

KEVIN:

They're rolling, because it's funny, and because nobody in that building has heard anything unrehearsed in twenty years. So then I hit them with the real stuff. I said, "Look at this room. You're all wearing outfits that cost more than most people's rent. We're at the Oscars, the only place where a person who makes twenty million dollars a movie can stand on stage and thank their third-grade drama teacher like she's personally responsible for their twelve-million-dollar paycheck. And we're all going to pretend that's normal."

The metallic ***CLANG*** *of a door opening.* ***OFFICER MARTINEZ*** *enters, escorting* ***ROB. ROB*** *is mid-thirties, wearing an ill-fitting prison jumpsuit that's slightly too big. He looks exhausted and humiliated, like he's trying to disappear into himself.*

***MARTINEZ** is no-nonsense and tired.*

MARTINEZ:

Alright, fresh fish. This is your home for the next however-many months your lawyer couldn't get you out of. Top bunk. Commissary's Thursdays. Lights out at ten. Rec time is eight to nine if you don't piss me off. Any questions?

***ROB** shakes his head, not making eye contact.*

MARTINEZ:

Great. Try not to kill each other. I've got enough paperwork as it is.

She exits.

*The door **CLANGS** shut. **ROB** stands frozen, staring at the cell. **KEVIN** watches him like a cat observing a new toy. He doesn't rush.*

KEVIN:

Hey.

***ROB** doesn't respond.*

KEVIN:

Hey, man. Welcome to the Ritz-Carlton, Block C edition. I'm KEVIN.

***ROB** finally looks at him, then quickly away.*

ROB *(barely audible)*:

Rob.

KEVIN:

Rob. Good to meet you. You need anything? Commissary's Thursday.

You'll want to put money on your books if you haven't already.

ROB:

I'm fine.

CHALK *(offstage)*:

Kevin, you gonna finish that story or leave us hanging all night?

KEVIN *(still watching **ROB**)*:

Yeah, yeah. Give the new guy a second.

***ROB** moves to the top bunk and starts making the bed with mechanical, precise movements, focusing on the task so he doesn't have to think about where he is.*

KEVIN *(to **ROB**)*:

First night's the hardest. It gets easier.

ROB *(sharper)*:

I said I'm fine.

*Beat. **KEVIN** raises his eyebrows: intrigued, not offended.*

KEVIN *(to the tier)*:

Alright, where was I?

CLICKS:

The drama teacher line! You just roasted the whole front row!

KEVIN:

Right! So they're laughing, but it's getting nervous now, because they're starting to realize I'm not part of the show. And I can feel it shift: that moment where funny tips into dangerous. And that's when I leaned in. I said, "And in about twenty minutes, one of you is going to cry on camera. Real tears. You rehearsed them in the car. Your publicist told you which camera to look at. Your stylist made sure your mascara was waterproof. Nothing about this is spontaneous. But forty million people at home are going to feel something. And that's the trick, isn't it? You're so good at performing emotion that nobody notices you've stopped actually having any."

RADAR *(offstage)*:
Damn. You said that to their faces?

KEVIN:
To their faces. Live. And then I gave a shout-out to the fans.

CLICKS:
The fans?

KEVIN:
I said, "Shout-out to my friends on the internet. The fans. I love you guys. You spend sixteen hours a day telling me I'm a loser, but at least you're passionate! You're the only ones who actually watch the whole show! The people in this room leave as soon as their category is done. They're already in the car heading to an after-party where nobody eats and everybody lies. But the fans? They're ride-or-die. They watch every second so they can tell me exactly why I'm garbage. That's commitment. That's love."

CHALK *(offstage)*:
You went after the audience and the internet in the same breath. Bold.

KEVIN:
Go big or go home. Except I couldn't go home because I was about to go to jail. But then, then I hit the real stuff. The part that matters.

THE SAGE *(offstage)*:
What did you say?

KEVIN:

I told them the truth about their industry. I said, "You give speeches about courage. Standing ovations for courage. Awards for playing characters who had courage. But the moment someone actually takes a risk, a real risk, you blacklist them. You ghost them. You memory-hole them so fast it's like they never existed." I said, "You cry about representation on this stage and then you won't return a phone call from anyone who doesn't have an agent at one of three agencies. There are eight billion people on this planet and you keep casting the same forty of them. You've got a planet full of talent beating down the door, and you won't let them in because they didn't go to the right school, didn't know the right people, or didn't grow up in the right zip code. You call this a meritocracy? This isn't a meritocracy; this is a gated community with better lighting."

ROB *(despite himself, still facing away)*:

A gated community with better lighting.

***KEVIN** catches it: **ROB** repeating the line. Almost involuntary. Got him.*

THE SAGE *(offstage)*:

There's something profound about humor in that context. The court jester was historically the only person permitted to speak truth to power because the truth was wrapped in laughter. And laughter dissolves fear. If people can laugh at their leaders, they cannot revere them. And without reverence, power becomes transparent.

KEVIN:

Yes! That's exactly what I was doing up there, Sage. I told them, "This isn't about art. It's about protecting the hierarchy, making sure everybody knows who's on top and who's grateful to be invited. But here's the secret they don't want you to know: once you show people they're allowed to laugh at the people on the pedestal, the pedestal disappears. Once you laugh at something, you stop being intimidated by it. And that's why they hate people like me.

Not because I'm wrong, but because I'm funny. And funny is the one thing they can't control."

ROB *(quietly, still not turning)*:
And then they cut off the jester's head.

Beat. Everyone processes this.

KEVIN:
Sometimes. Yeah. But the joke survives. That's the thing about humor: it outlives the people who try to suppress it. Kill the comedian, and the joke still spreads. Lock me up, and the video still gets forty million views.

THE CRITIC:
And now you're in here. Real victory.

KEVIN:
The fact that they put me in a cage tells you they took it seriously. If it didn't matter, I'd still be walking around free.

RADAR *(offstage, quieter)*:
How'd they finally get you off?

KEVIN:
I saw the suits coming from both wings. Greg brought backup. And I knew I had maybe ten seconds. So I said, "Alright, alright. I'm going to prison now, probably. But you're going to be talking about this tomorrow. Check the hashtags. God bless the critics, God bless the crazies, and somebody please feed my cat while I'm in county."

CLICKS:
Feed your cat?

KEVIN:

You go big, you gotta go human. Forty million people just watched me dismantle Hollywood, and the last thing I say is about my cat. That's what people remember: the human moment inside the chaos. And then security reaches me, gentle and professional because the cameras are still rolling, and as they're walking me off, I lean into the mic one last time and say, "I'd like to thank my agent… oh wait, I don't have one. That's the point." And I dropped the mic. Actually dropped it. You could hear it hit the stage. And I let them walk me off.

CLICKS:

That clip alone probably got ten million views.

KEVIN:

Twelve. Just the walk-off line. The full seven minutes? Forty million and counting. Memes, remixes, people doing dramatic readings, and animated versions. I became the guy who crashed the Oscars and told the truth.

***ROB** has stopped making his bed. He's sitting on the edge of his bunk, facing away but completely still, listening.*

CHALK *(offstage)*:

I've seen guys come in here with stories. Most of them get smaller every time they tell them. Yours keeps getting bigger. Which means it's either real or you're the best liar on this tier.

KEVIN:

Got the video right here, Chalk. Contraband phone. I'll show anyone who wants to see it.

CHALK:

I'll believe it when I see it.

The lights begin to dim as evening approaches.

MARTINEZ *(offstage, distant)*:
Lights out in thirty! Wrap it up!

KEVIN:
Alright, gentlemen. You heard the lady.

CLICKS:
Night, Kevin! Welcome, new guy!

THE SAGE:
May your dreams bring clarity.

THE CRITIC:
Finally. Silence.

KEVIN:
Night, Critic.

KEVIN *settles onto his bunk. The lights continue to dim. Prison sounds in the distance: doors, voices, and footsteps.* ***ROB*** *is still sitting up, arms around his knees.*

ROB *(quietly, after a long pause)*:
Did you really do all that?

KEVIN *(from his bunk)*:
Every word.

ROB:
Why?

KEVIN:

Why'd they let me? Or why'd I do it?

ROB:

Why'd you do it. You had to know you'd get caught.

Long pause.

KEVIN:

Yeah, I knew. But the video would get out. The laughter would happen. And once that starts, you can't stop it. You can arrest me, but the idea's already out there. Once you show people they're allowed to laugh at the people they've been taught to admire, you can't make them un-see that.

ROB:

Was it worth it?

KEVIN:

Ask me in two months when I get out.

Long pause. The lights are very dim now.

ROB:

You have the video?

KEVIN:

Saved on a phone that violates about six different prison rules. Want to see it tomorrow?

ROB:

...Yeah. Okay.

KEVIN:

Get some sleep, Rob.

Very long pause. Almost complete darkness now except for a faint glow: moonlight through a high window.

ROB:

Kevin?

KEVIN:

Yeah?

ROB:

Do you really think you changed anything? With all that?

KEVIN *(genuine)*:

I think I reminded forty million people that they have a voice. Did it change the industry? No. Did it change the people watching? Maybe a few of them. And sometimes that's all you can do: plant the seed and see what grows.

ROB:

That's pretty optimistic for a guy in prison.

KEVIN:

Optimism's a choice, and cynicism's exactly what they want from us. So I choose the opposite.

Very long pause. The darkness is almost complete.

ROB *(so quietly it's almost a whisper)*:

I don't think I matter anymore.

Silence. ***KEVIN*** *has heard it. He lets it sit. Then:*

KEVIN:

Get some sleep, Rob.

Complete silence. Then, from the darkness:

RADAR *(offstage, very quietly)*:
New guy's hurting, Kevin.

KEVIN *(whispered)*:
I know.

Blackout.

END SCENE 1

ACT ONE: SCENE TWO

SCENE 2: THE CRIMES

Morning light. Harsh fluorescent quality. Breakfast has come and gone. ***KEVIN*** *is doing push-ups on the floor.* ***ROB*** *sits on his bunk, staring at nothing. He hasn't slept well: it shows.*

KEVIN *(counting)*:
...forty-eight, forty-nine, fifty.

He stands, barely winded.

KEVIN:
Morning. How'd you sleep?

Nothing from ***ROB.***

KEVIN:
You eat breakfast?

ROB *(finally)*:
Wasn't hungry.

KEVIN:
You gotta eat. If you don't, the guards think you're planning something: a

hunger strike, suicide watch. Trust me, you don't want that attention.

ROB *nods slightly but doesn't move.*

RADAR *(offstage)*:

Yo Kevin, you showing new guy the video today?

KEVIN:

That's the plan. Rob, you still want to see it?

ROB *(after a pause)*:

...Sure.

KEVIN *glances at the cell door before crouching in the cramped space behind the toilet. He digs his fingernails into the mortar of a corner brick until it gives way. Behind the masonry sits a small* ***PHONE*** *wrapped in plastic. He pulls it free, frantically unwrapping the layers until the screen glows to life against his palm.*

KEVIN:

Takes forever to boot. Burner phone. So while we wait, what are you in for?

ROB:

No.

KEVIN:

Come on. We're cellmates. We're gonna know everything about each other eventually. I showed you mine.

ROB:

I didn't ask you to.

KEVIN:

Fair. But you listened. You even asked questions.

ROB:

It's embarrassing.

KEVIN:

I impersonated a stagehand using a headset from Best Buy and crashed live television. Embarrassing is my whole thing.

Long pause. ***ROB*** *stares at his hands.*

ROB *(quietly)*:

I dropped fake money from a plane.

Beat. ***KEVIN*** *looks up from the phone.*

KEVIN:

I'm sorry, what?

ROB:

I rented a plane. And I dropped fake hundred-dollar bills over the city, with my face and phone number on them.

KEVIN *stares at him.*

KEVIN:

You rented a plane.

ROB:

Yes.

KEVIN:

To drop fake money.

ROB:
Yes.

KEVIN:
With your face on the bills.

ROB:
And my phone number. And my real estate company.

KEVIN *(starting to grin)*:
That's… that's fucking genius.

ROB:
It caused a fifteen-car pileup.

KEVIN:
Okay, so it's flawed genius.

ROB:
People got hurt. Not seriously, but still. Property damage. Traffic chaos. Reckless endangerment, fraud, and FAA violations.

KEVIN:
But why? Why would you do that?

ROB *(defensive)*:
I'm a real estate agent. Everyone's doing online ads, social media, and billboards. I needed something people would remember.

KEVIN:
Mission accomplished.

ROB:

My wife won't talk to me. My clients dropped me. My reputation is destroyed. So yeah, they'll remember me: as the idiot who made it rain fake money and caused a highway pileup.

CLICKS *(offstage)*:

Wait, is new guy the "Money Rain Guy?"

ROB *(groaning)*:

Oh god.

CLICKS:

I saw that video! Cars stopping on the highway, people jumping out grabbing bills... that was everywhere. That was you?

ROB:

Can we please not...

CLICKS:

Dude, you went mega-viral. That clip was on every platform for like two weeks straight.

CHALK *(offstage)*:

Hold up. New guy is Money Rain Rob?

ROB:

Please stop calling me that.

CHALK:

I remember that. My niece sent me the link. Said, "Uncle, you gotta see this idiot." No offense.

ROB:

None taken. She's right.

THE SAGE *(offstage)*:

A modern Icarus. Paper wings of currency.

THE CRITIC:

A modern idiot with a pilot's license.

KEVIN *(ignoring them, focused on **ROB**)*:

How much did the whole thing cost you?

ROB:

Fifteen hundred for the plane. Two grand for printing. Maybe thirty-five hundred total.

***KEVIN** is typing on the phone.*

KEVIN:

"Real estate agent drops fake money from plane." Here we go. Holy shit. Eight million views on the main video, plus re-posts, news coverage, and compilations.

ROB:

I know the numbers. I don't need to hear them.

KEVIN:

You spent thirty-five hundred bucks and got maybe eighteen million impressions. Do you know what that costs in advertising? You got the deal of the century. You just didn't capitalize on it.

ROB:

Because I got arrested.

KEVIN:

Details.

ROB:

Details? I'm in prison.

KEVIN:

Temporarily. And when you get out, you're not going back to being some nobody real estate agent. You're the guy who made it rain. The guy with the story.

ROB:

The guy with a criminal record.

KEVIN:

The guy people remember. And attention is currency. You and me, we did the same thing: pulled stunts that got us arrested. But those stunts also got us seen. And memorable is valuable.

ROB:

Valuable. Right. Tell that to my wife. Tell that to the client who just dropped me. Tell that to every person in my life who thinks I'm a joke.

KEVIN:

I'm telling it to you, because you're the one who needs to hear it. Think about it: you've got the ideas and the audacity. I've got the performance skills and the timing. Together we could build something: a production company or a marketing agency. Something where we help people get attention without getting arrested.

***ROB** turns and looks at **KEVIN** for the first time in the conversation. Really looks at him.*

ROB:

You want to start a company. With me.

KEVIN:

Yeah.

ROB:

You want to start a company with a guy who can't keep his marriage together, who just lost his biggest client, and who's sitting in a prison cell because he thought raining money from a plane was a good marketing strategy.

KEVIN:

When you put it like that...

ROB:

There's no other way to put it. That's what it is. You don't even know me. You've known me for less than twenty-four hours and you're already planning my future like I'm some project you can fix.

KEVIN:

I'm not trying to fix you.

ROB:

Then what are you trying to do? Because from where I'm sitting, it sounds like you need a partner more than I do. It sounds like you need someone to validate your big plan so you don't have to sit with the fact that you're stuck in here just like the rest of us.

That lands. ***KEVIN's*** *smile falters, just for a second.*

CHALK *(offstage, quiet)*:

Hmmm. New guy's got teeth.

KEVIN:

That's not what this is.

ROB:

Isn't it? You've been here four months. You've had four months to pitch this idea to someone, and nobody's bitten. So the new guy walks in, the guy who's scared and broken and desperate, and you think: there's my mark. There's someone who'll say yes because he doesn't have anything else.

*Silence on the tier. Even **THE CRITIC** has nothing.*

KEVIN *(carefully)*:

Is that what you think this is? A con?

ROB:

I think you're a guy who crashed an awards show for attention, and now you're looking for the next performance. I just don't want to be part of the act.

*Long beat. **KEVIN** holds **ROB's** gaze. Something genuine breaks through the charm.*

He picks up the phone and holds it out.

KEVIN:

You still want to see the video?

***ROB** hesitates, then takes it. **KEVIN** climbs up and sits next to him on the top bunk. They watch. The light from the **SCREEN** plays on their faces.*

KEVIN:

That's me walking on. Watch the audience. See their faces? They have no idea what's happening.

Long pause as they watch.

ROB:

Holy shit.

KEVIN:

Right?

ROB:

You really did this.

KEVIN:

I really did this.

ROB:

The woman in the third row. She's really laughing.

KEVIN:

Hardest I've ever made anyone laugh. And she's somebody, which made it better.

They watch in silence for a moment. ***ROB*** *is absorbed.*

ROB:

This is actually incredible.

KEVIN:

Thank you.

ROB:

It's also completely reckless and you deserved to get arrested.

KEVIN:

Sure, sure.

ROB:

But it's incredible.

They watch a moment longer. Then ***ROB*** *hands the phone back. He climbs down to the floor. The spell breaks. His walls go back up.*

ROB:

Doesn't change anything, though. What you did, that was you. Your stunt. Your talent. I'm not you. I'm not a performer. I'm a real estate agent who had one stupid idea and destroyed his life with it.

KEVIN:

One stupid idea that got eight million views.

ROB:

One stupid idea that got me here. And I don't get to spin that into a comeback story. I'm not charming enough, I'm not quick enough, I'm not whatever you are. I'm just a guy who fucked up. And the sooner I accept that, the sooner I can figure out how to survive the next eight to twelve months without losing my mind.

He climbs back up to his bunk and turns toward the wall. Conversation over.

KEVIN:

Rob...

ROB:

I'm done talking about it.

KEVIN *sits there. For once, he doesn't push. He puts the phone away and lies back on his bunk. The silence is heavy.*

CLICKS *(offstage, quietly)*:

He didn't go for it, huh?

KEVIN:

Not yet.

CHALK:

"Not yet." I've heard that before. Guy last year had a food truck plan. Was gonna revolutionize the industry. His cellmate was gonna be his sous chef. Know where they are now?

KEVIN:

Where?

CHALK:

One's back in here. Other one manages a Wendy's. Not exactly a revolution.

THE CRITIC:

Chalk with the bedtime story. Heartwarming as always.

CHALK:

I'm not trying to be mean. I'm trying to be honest. Plans made in here don't survive out there. The world doesn't care about your prison epiphanies.

KEVIN:

Maybe not. But some plans are different.

CHALK:

They all think they're different, Kevin.

That sits. ***KEVIN*** *doesn't have a comeback for it.*

RADAR *(offstage, after a pause)*:

He watched the whole video though. Didn't look away once.

KEVIN:
Yeah. He did.

RADAR:
That's something.

__KEVIN__ looks up at the underside of __ROB's__ bunk.

KEVIN:
Yeah. That's something.

The lights begin to fade.

THE SAGE *(quietly)*:
The seed does not announce itself when it takes root.

__KEVIN__ lies back. Above him, __ROB__ is facing the wall. Not asleep. Both of them are awake in the growing dark, thinking. The distance between their bunks feels immense.

Blackout.

END SCENE 2

ACT ONE: SCENE THREE

SCENE 3: THE PROVOCATION

Days later. Late afternoon: that particular light that makes everything feel heavy. The cell has subtle signs of time passing: ***ROB'S*** *few possessions arranged on his bunk area, a routine established.* ***ROB*** *is lying on the top bunk, staring at the ceiling. He's holding two opened* ***ENVELOPES. KEVIN*** *is on his bunk reading a contraband paperback. The silence between them has a practiced quality; they've learned each other's rhythms. But something is different today.* ***ROB*** *has been up there since morning.*

KEVIN *(without looking up)*:
You've been up there since breakfast.

Nothing from ***ROB.***

KEVIN:
You eat today?

Nothing.

KEVIN:
Rob.

ROB *(flat)*:

Court date got pushed back. Again.

KEVIN:

How far back?

ROB:

Three months. Minimum. Which means I'm in here longer than anyone told me. And my biggest client. They sent a letter.

He reads from it, voice dead.

ROB:

"We regret that we can no longer be associated with someone who has demonstrated such poor judgment and reckless behavior."

*He **CRUMPLES** both letters together.*

ROB:

Fifty thousand dollar commission. Gone.

KEVIN:

Rob...

ROB:

Don't.

KEVIN:

I wasn't going to...

ROB:

Yeah you were. You were going to tell me this is an opportunity. That this is just a setback. That I should reframe it. That's what you do. That's all you do.

***KEVIN** closes his book.*

KEVIN:

Okay. What do you want me to say?

ROB:

Nothing. I want you to say nothing. I want silence. But I can't have that because I'm locked in a six-by-eight box with someone who treats every disaster like it's material for a pitch meeting.

KEVIN:

That's not fair.

ROB *(sitting up)*:

Isn't it? Because you've been pretty happy about being in here. This is all just a story to you. A chapter in the Kevin Richardson comeback narrative. But me? I'm losing everything. And you keep telling me it's all going to work out like you have any idea what that feels like.

KEVIN:

You think I don't know what that feels like?

ROB:

I think you're really good at pretending you don't.

KEVIN *(jaw tightening)*:

And you're really good at feeling sorry for yourself.

*The temperature drops. **ROB** climbs down from his bunk.*

ROB:

What did you just say?

KEVIN *(standing)*:

I said you've been wallowing. I get it: you're going through shit. But at some point you have to decide: are you gonna let it destroy you, or are you gonna do something about it?

ROB:

And what exactly should I do from inside a prison cell?

KEVIN:

You could stop acting like a victim and start acting like someone who made a choice. You chose to rent that plane. You chose to drop that money. Nobody did this to you.

***ROB** takes a step toward **KEVIN**. They're face to face now.*

ROB:

You don't know what you're talking about.

KEVIN:

You wanted to be seen. You wanted to matter. You wanted to be more than just some safe, boring real estate agent. Well, congratulations. You got your wish. And you hate it because it didn't come with the outcome you wanted.

ROB:

Fuck you!

KEVIN:

You too buddy! You think you're the only one who's lost things? I had opportunities. Connections. People starting to take me seriously. And I threw it all away for seven minutes of glory.

ROB:

At least you chose your suffering. At least you knew what you were walking into.

KEVIN:

And you didn't? You didn't know that dropping fake money from a plane might have consequences?

ROB *(shouting)*:

Then what's the point? What's the point of taking risks if they just destroy your life?

KEVIN *(shouting back)*:

The point is you tried! The point is you did something instead of spending your whole life wondering what if!

ROB:

I don't want to be alive like this!

***ROB** shoves **KEVIN**. Hard. **KEVIN** stumbles back against his bunk.*

CHALK *(offstage)*:

Oh shit...

RADAR:

Yo, yo, yo...

ROB *(advancing)*:

You want to keep going? You want to keep telling me how to feel?

KEVIN *(straightening up, something dangerous in his eyes)*:

Yeah. Let's go. You want to get real? Let's get real. You're not mad at me. You're not even mad at the system. You're mad at yourself. Because deep down, you know that stunt was the most interesting thing you've ever done. And you hate that. You hate that the best moment of your life is also the worst moment of your life.

ROB:

Shut up...

KEVIN:

Your wife married a safe guy. A boring guy. And the one time you did something unexpected, something alive, it destroyed everything. And now you don't know who to be: Safe Rob or Interesting Rob. Because you can't be both.

ROB:

I said shut up...

KEVIN:

And you know what? Part of you is relieved she's pulling away. Because now you don't have to pretend anymore. Now you get to figure out who you are without someone watching.

***ROB** is shaking.*

ROB *(low, dangerous)*:

You want to talk about my marriage? Let's talk about your relationships. Where's your wife, Kevin? Where's your family? Oh wait: you don't have any. Because nobody wants to come home to someone who can't take anything seriously.

***KEVIN** tenses.*

ROB:

Yeah. How's that feel? Not so fun when someone's picking apart your life. Under all those jokes, you're just as scared as I am. You're just better at performing. But in here? You can't perform your way out. And that terrifies you. You know what I think? I think you like being in here. Out there, you're just another failed comedian with a viral clip. But in here, you're the legend. You're somebody. This cage is the only place you've ever mattered.

The tier is dead silent.

KEVIN *(very quietly)*:
Careful.

ROB:
Or what?

*Long beat. Then **KEVIN** starts to laugh. Not nervous: real.*

ROB:
What's so funny?

KEVIN:
You. You think anger scares me? You think I don't know I use humor because the alternative is screaming? You think I don't lie awake at night thinking about everything I lost?

ROB:
Then why are you so happy all the time?

KEVIN:
Because the alternative is being you! Lying on my bunk all day, feeling sorry for myself, giving them the satisfaction of breaking me!

*He's right in **ROB'S** face now.*

KEVIN:
They can lock me up. Take my freedom. Take my career. But they can't

take my ability to laugh at them. And that drives them insane.

ROB:
That's not power. That's delusion.

KEVIN:
Then why are you so mad? Why does it bother you that I'm not as miserable as you want me to be?

ROB:
Because it's fake!

KEVIN:
It's survival!

Both breathing hard. Inches apart.

ROB:
I don't believe you. I think you're just as broken as the rest of us. You're just too proud to admit it.

KEVIN:
Oh, you want to talk about broken? Let's talk about broken. Let's talk about how your father was a door-to-door condom salesman who had no sense to use his own product. And here you are.

The tier erupts.

CHALK:
Damn!

CLICKS:
Bro!

RADAR:
Sounds like he was selling some good ass rubbers.

ROB'S *face goes white, then red.*

ROB *(deadly quiet)*:
What did you just say?

KEVIN:
You spent your whole life trying to be better than your dad. Respectable. Successful. And you ended up in the same place.

ROB *lunges. They crash into the bunk, grappling. Not skilled fighting: desperate, clumsy, two men releasing something they've been holding in.*

CHALK *(offstage)*:
Fight! Fight!

They break apart, circling in the small space.

ROB:
You want to talk about fathers? Where was your dad when you were bombing auditions? When you needed someone to believe in you? He thought you were a joke, didn't he? And you know what: he was right. You're in prison.

KEVIN'S *face hardens.*

KEVIN:
At least I had a father who cared enough to have an opinion...

ROB *swings.* ***KEVIN*** *ducks. They crash together again: more desperate than violent.*

KEVIN *(grappling)*:
Your wife left because you're boring!

ROB:
You're alone because nobody can stand you!

KEVIN:
You're alone because nobody knows you!

They break apart.

From offstage:

OFFICER MARTINEZ *(storming toward the cell)*:
What the hell is going on in here?!

She reaches the bars. Both men on opposite sides of the cell, worked up, breathing hard.

MARTINEZ:
I said what is going on?

CLICKS:
Officer Martinez, you can't shut this down now!

THE CRITIC:
For once, something interesting is happening.

THE SAGE *(offstage)*:
Perhaps this conflict needs to reach its natural conclusion, Officer.

MARTINEZ:
Jenkins, if you go philosophical on me right now, I swear to God…

*She looks at **KEVIN** and **ROB**. Then at the tier. No other guards visible. She makes a decision.*

MARTINEZ:

Three minutes. And if anyone asks, I was in Block D. This stays verbal. If you actually hit each other again, you're both going to solitary.

She leans against the wall near the bars. Arms crossed. Watching.

MARTINEZ:

Finish what you started.

*Beat. **KEVIN** and **ROB** lock eyes. The energy shifts; it's not about violence anymore. It's about truth.*

KEVIN:

Your turn. Don't hold back.

ROB *(slowly)*:

You think you're helping people. With your jokes. Your stunts. Your "speaking truth to power." But you're not helping anyone. You're just feeding your own ego. Forty million people watched your video. Did it change anything? Did one single thing shift? Or did people just laugh, share it, and move on while you're sitting in here pretending it meant something?

Beat.

KEVIN *(quietly)*:

That actually hurt.

ROB:

Good. Your turn.

KEVIN:

You're not mad that your stunt failed. You're mad that it worked. You got what you wanted: attention, recognition, everyone knowing your name. And it terrified you. Because the moment everyone was looking at you, you hid. You called it a mistake. You apologized. You tried to make yourself small again. Because being visible? That's terrifying. And you're not brave enough for it.

*Silence. Something shifts in **ROB**.*

ROB *(quieter)*:

Maybe I'm not.

KEVIN:

And maybe I'm not helping anyone either. Maybe I'm just a narcissist with delusions of grandeur.

The anger is draining out of both of them. What's left is something rawer. Exhaustion. Recognition.

ROB:

Your dad really thought you were a joke?

KEVIN:

Haven't talked to him in three years.

ROB:

My dad... he was an insurance salesman. Bad at it. We were always broke. I spent my whole childhood watching him fail.

KEVIN:

Is that why you went into real estate? Stability?

ROB:

I wanted to be his opposite. And then I dropped fake money from a plane. Like father, like son.

Beat.

ROB:

That condom salesman line was fucked up.

KEVIN:

I'm sorry... But that was funny!

ROB *Ignores him.*

ROB:

The stuff about my wife was probably true.

KEVIN:

Probably.

Long pause. ***MARTINEZ*** *is still watching from the bars. She hasn't moved.*

MARTINEZ *(after a moment)*:

You two done?

KEVIN:

Yeah. We're done.

MARTINEZ:

Good.

She doesn't leave. She looks at ***ROB.***

MARTINEZ:

Wilson.

ROB:

Yes, ma'am.

MARTINEZ:

I've been working this block for nine years. I've watched a lot of men come through here. Most of them do their time staring at the ceiling, counting days, waiting for it to be over. They leave exactly the way they came in. Nothing changes. Nothing grows.

She looks between them.

MARTINEZ:

Every once in a while, someone decides to use the time. To actually do something with it. Those are the ones who don't come back.

Beat.

MARTINEZ:

You two just screamed the truth at each other for five minutes. Most people go their whole lives without doing that. So whatever this is, this thing you're fighting about, this plan, this partnership, whatever: figure it out. Because the clock's ticking and you don't get this time back.

She straightens up.

MARTINEZ:

And if I hear one more sound from this cell tonight, you're both going to solitary. Understood?

KEVIN:

Understood.

ROB:

Yes, ma'am.

She walks away. Her footsteps recede. ***KEVIN*** *and* ***ROB*** *stand in the small cell, looking at each other. The fight is over. Neither of them won. Neither of them lost.*

ROB:

You're an asshole.

KEVIN:

You're not wrong.

Beat.

ROB:

You're funny when you're mean. You know that?

KEVIN:

You're funny when you're angry. That stuff about me liking prison? About this cage being the only place I've mattered? That was sharp. That was good timing.

ROB:

I wasn't trying to be funny. I was trying to hurt you.

KEVIN:

Exactly. That's what makes it funny. The best comedy is just truth with attitude.

ROB:

I've never thought of myself as funny.

KEVIN:
Most funny people don't.

***ROB** climbs back up to his bunk. **KEVIN** sits on his. The lights begin to dim.*

MARTINEZ *(offstage, distant)*:
Lights out!

Darkness settling. The tier is quiet; everyone is processing what they witnessed.

CHALK *(offstage, after a long silence)*:
Kevin.

KEVIN:
Yeah, Chalk.

CHALK:
The food truck guy and his sous chef. They didn't have what you two have.

KEVIN:
What do we have?

CHALK:
I don't know yet. But it's something.

*That sits in the dark. From **CHALK**, that's enormous.*

THE CRITIC *(offstage)*:
I'm not crying. Shut up.

CLICKS:
Nobody said you were crying, Critic.

THE CRITIC:

Good. Keep it that way.

Almost complete darkness now.

ROB:

Kevin?

KEVIN:

Yeah?

Long pause.

ROB:

The Viral Outlaws.

KEVIN: What?

ROB:

That's what you'd call it. The company. The Viral Outlaws. We went viral. We broke the rules. We're outlaws.

Silence.

KEVIN:

Where'd that come from?

ROB:

I've been thinking about it. Since you showed me the video. I told you I wasn't interested and then I couldn't stop thinking about it. That's been pissing me off for days. That's half of why I was angry.

Beat.

KEVIN:

You've been mad because you want to say yes.

ROB:

I've been mad because saying yes means admitting this might actually be something. And if it's something, it can fail. And I don't know if I can survive another failure.

Long silence.

KEVIN:

It might fail.

ROB:

I know.

KEVIN:

It might fail spectacularly.

ROB:

I know.

KEVIN:

You in anyway?

Very long pause.

ROB:

Yeah. I'm in.

Silence in the dark.

RADAR *(offstage, very quietly)*:

He said it.

KEVIN *(in the darkness)*:

Partners?

ROB:

Partners. Now shut up and let me sleep. Martinez wasn't kidding about solitary.

In the darkness, ***KEVIN*** *smiles. We can't see it. But we know.*

Complete darkness. Complete silence.

Blackout.

END SCENE 3

END ACT ONE

INTERMISSION

ACT TWO: SCENE ONE

SCENE 1: THE PLAN

*Days later. The cell has shifted. Papers are scattered on **KEVIN'S** bunk: notes on scraps, commissary napkins, the backs of envelopes. A makeshift war room. The energy between **KEVIN** and **ROB** is different from Act One: looser, more direct. They've stopped being polite. **ROB** sits on his bunk with a commissary notebook, writing. **KEVIN** paces, talking through ideas.*

KEVIN:

Okay. Tagline. "We went viral. We went to prison. Now we help YOU go viral without the prison part."

ROB:

Too long.

KEVIN:

It's a tagline, not a novel.

ROB:

It's three sentences. A tagline is one sentence. Or less.

KEVIN:

Fine. What's yours?

ROB:

"Go viral without going to prison."

Beat.

KEVIN:
That's better.

ROB:
I know it is.

KEVIN:
Don't get cocky. What about services? We need specifics.

ROB:
Stunt design and execution. Controlled chaos: events big enough to get coverage but not big enough to get indicted.

KEVIN:
I like "controlled chaos." That's good.

ROB:
Second: crisis management. People who've already fucked up. Scandals, mistakes, public embarrassments. We help them own it instead of hiding from it.

KEVIN:
Crisis PR for the shameless. Love it.

ROB:
Don't call it that.

KEVIN:
Why not?

ROB:

Because clients who've been publicly humiliated don't want to hire a company that calls them shameless. They want to feel like we understand what they're going through.

***KEVIN** stops pacing. Looks at **ROB**.*

KEVIN:

That's... actually a really good point.

ROB:

I sold houses to people who were terrified of the biggest purchase of their lives. You don't close that deal by being clever. You close it by making them feel safe.

KEVIN:

Okay. So what do we call it?

ROB:

Reputation rehabilitation. Or just "narrative strategy." We help people rewrite their story.

KEVIN:

Third service: content production. Podcasts, web series, social media campaigns.

ROB:

Fourth: speaking engagements. We tell our story to companies, colleges. "How we turned failure into a business."

KEVIN:

Yes! We're not just consultants, we're proof. Walking, talking proof that...

ROB:
Stop.

KEVIN:
What?

ROB:
You're pitching me. I'm already in. Save the performance for people who haven't heard it.

CHALK *(offstage)*:
He's got a point, Kevin.

KEVIN:
Nobody asked you, Chalk.

CHALK:
Free advice. You're welcome.

CLICKS *(offstage)*:
Can I ask a real question?

KEVIN: Shoot.

CLICKS:
Who's your first client? You've got services, you've got a name, but you've got no portfolio. No case studies. No proof you can deliver. How do you get someone to take a chance on two ex-cons with a website and a prison backstory?

Beat. ***KEVIN*** *and* ***ROB*** *look at each other.*

ROB:

That's a good question.

KEVIN:

WE'RE the case study. Our own viral moments. We show how we'd do it differently with the knowledge we have now. A retrospective. "Here's what we did wrong and what we learned."

ROB:

That only works if people still remember who we are when we get out. Your video's what, six months old already?

***KEVIN** tenses. **ROB** has touched a nerve, probably knowingly.*

KEVIN:

It's still at forty million views.

ROB:

Forty million views and zero growth. I'm not attacking you. I'm asking the question a client would ask. "What have you done lately?"

CHALK *(offstage)*:

He's right. People forget fast. I've watched guys in here ride their fifteen minutes like it's gonna last forever. It doesn't.

KEVIN:

So what are you saying? That we're already irrelevant?

ROB:

I'm saying the video is our foot in the door, not the whole house. We need something new. Something we CREATE, not something we're coasting on.

KEVIN:

Like what?

ROB:

I don't know yet. But I know that leading with "remember that thing from eight months ago" is a losing pitch.

***KEVIN** sits down on his bunk. This is the first time **ROB** has pushed the strategy harder than **KEVIN**.*

KEVIN:

Okay. So we need a launch moment. Something that announces the company and proves what we can do at the same time.

ROB:

Now you're thinking.

KEVIN:

When did you become the boss of this operation?

ROB:

When you needed someone to tell you your first draft was sloppy. That's what partners are for.

RADAR *(offstage)*:

I like this version of Rob.

THE CRITIC:

Marginally less pathetic than the moping version, I'll grant you that.

KEVIN:

Alright. Let's role-play. I'm a potential client. You pitch me. Convince me to hire us.

ROB:

Why me?

KEVIN:

Because you sold houses. Same skill set. You're just selling us instead of property.

ROB:

That's completely different.

KEVIN:

Try. Go.

***ROB** stands. Uncomfortable.*

ROB:

Hi. I'm Rob Wilson from The Viral Outlaws.

KEVIN *(as a female client)*:

Never heard of you.

ROB:

Good. That means you haven't heard anything bad about us yet.

*Small beat. **KEVIN** drops character for a second, surprised.*

KEVIN *(as a female client)*:

There's a million marketing companies. Why would I hire you?

ROB:

Because every other agency is going to promise you results. They'll show you graphs and case studies and analytics dashboards. But none of them have ever actually DONE it. None of them have ever stood in front of millions of people and said something that mattered. My partner and I did. And we both ended up in prison for it.

KEVIN *(as a female client)*:

You're criminals?

ROB:

We're entrepreneurs who learned the hard way where the line is. Which means we know exactly how close you can get to it without crossing it. We're not here to play it safe. We're here to make you impossible to ignore.

***KEVIN** drops character. Staring at **ROB**.*

KEVIN:

Where did THAT come from?

ROB:

I don't know. I was just talking.

KEVIN:

That was the pitch. THAT. Right there. You sounded like you believed it.

ROB:

I think I do. Believe it. I just... hadn't heard myself say it out loud before.

CLICKS *(offstage)*:

Yo, Rob, that was legit. You came in with a hook, handled the objection, flipped the liability into a selling point. That's clean.

ROB:

Thanks... Clicks.

CLICKS:

One note though. You need a call to action. Something at the end that moves them from interested to committed. "Here's what happens next" energy.

ROB:
Like what?

CLICKS:
Like, "Give us thirty days and a story worth telling. We'll give you a moment nobody forgets." Something you can put on the website, on a slide deck, on a business card.

KEVIN *(to* ***ROB****)*:
He's good.

ROB *(to* ***KEVIN****)*:
He's very good. Now do yours. I want to hear it.

KEVIN *stands. Instantly shifts into performance mode. Smooth, charismatic, practiced. Which is everything he's not.*

KEVIN:
Hi, I'm Kevin Richardson, co-founder of The Viral Outlaws. You know that video of the guy who crashed the biggest awards show on television and did seven minutes of unscripted comedy to forty million people? That was me. International headlines, cultural moment, and yes, six months in federal prison. But here's what I learned: attention isn't luck. It's architecture. And most people are too afraid to build anything tall enough to be seen. My partner and I know how to create moments that break through the noise without breaking the law. So if you're ready to stop being invisible, let's talk.

He sits.

KEVIN:
Too much?

ROB:

No. It's good. It's really good. But it's all you.

KEVIN:

What do you mean?

ROB:

"That was me." "I learned." "My partner and I." Where am I in that pitch? Where's the money rain? Where's the guy who spent thirty-five hundred dollars and got eighteen million impressions? You're selling Kevin Richardson. You're not selling The Viral Outlaws.

Beat. ***KEVIN*** *opens his mouth, then closes it.*

ROB:

This has to be BOTH of us or it doesn't work. We're not your company with me as a sidekick. We're partners. Equal billing. Your story AND my story. The performer and the strategist. The guy who took the stage and the guy who made it rain.

KEVIN:

You're right.

ROB:

I know I'm right.

KEVIN:

When did you get so assertive?

ROB:

When I stopped being afraid of you.

That lands. ***KEVIN*** *nods: genuine respect.*

KEVIN:

Okay. So we redo the pitch. Together. Both stories. Equal weight.

ROB:

And we need a portfolio piece. Something we've actually produced. Not just our own stories: something for someone else. Proof we can do for others what we accidentally did for ourselves.

CHALK *(offstage)*:

How are you gonna produce anything from inside a cell?

ROB:

We plan it. Design it. Have it ready so that the day Kevin gets out, he can execute it.

KEVIN:

Wait, I'm executing it alone?

ROB:

You're out in five weeks. I'm here for months after that. So yeah. You're the legs. I'm the brain calling shots from in here.

KEVIN:

Calling shots from prison. That's very Godfather of you.

ROB:

Focus. Who do we know who needs help? Someone whose situation we understand. Someone who's been publicly embarrassed, made a mistake, needs to rebuild.

Silence while they think. Then:

RADAR *(offstage)*:

What about that comedian? The one who got canceled for the post. Kevin, you told us about her last month.

KEVIN:

Sarah Glass. She made a joke about a senator and they came after her. Lost her Netflix deal, her agent dropped her.

ROB:

Do you know her?

KEVIN:

I know people who know her. We ran in some of the same circles before I ended up in here.

CLICKS (offstage):

Hold up. Her name is Glass. And she got shattered.

Beat. ***KEVIN*** *and* ***ROB*** *look at each other. Something clicking.*

CLICKS:

That's not a setback. That's a campaign.

ROB:

Bulletproof Glass.

KEVIN:

That's the comeback. That's the whole thing right there.

ROB:

But we don't write it. We don't script her. We give her the stage and let her tell it in her own words. What happened. What it cost her. Why she's still here.

KEVIN:

No spin. No PR clean-up. Just Sarah Glass, unscripted, saying what she actually wants to say. The thing she's been afraid to say because everyone told her to stay quiet and wait for it to blow over.

ROB:

"Waiting for it to blow over" is how careers die. She needs to move NOW.

CLICKS:

He's right. Authenticity outperforms produced content every time. You let her be real, it goes further than anything you could write for her.

ROB:

She's your first call. When you get out. Day one. You walk in with the concept, the name, the whole framework. You don't ask her if she needs help. You show her we already started.

KEVIN:

And if she says no?

ROB:

She's not going to say no.

KEVIN:

Rob...

ROB:

She's NOT. Think about it. Her Netflix deal is gone. Her agent dropped her. Every day she stays quiet, people forget her a little more. She's watching her career expire in real time and nobody's offering her a way back. We're not cold-calling with a sales pitch. We're showing up with a lifeline. "Bulletproof Glass." Her name. Her story. Her voice. She'd have to be out of her mind to turn that down.

KEVIN:
You really believe that.

ROB:
I watched clients lose houses because they waited too long to act. Hesitated while the market moved. Told themselves next month would be better. It's never better. The window closes. Sarah Glass has a window right now, and it's closing. We can save her career.

CHALK (offstage):
That's a nice speech. But what if she does say no?

ROB:
Then we find the next person who needs saving. There's no shortage.

CHALK:
There never is.

RADAR (offstage):
But she's not going to say no.

CHALK:
Probably not.

RADAR:
Was that encouragement, Chalk?

CHALK:
It was an observation. Don't read into it.

THE CRITIC *(offstage)*:
This is all very inspiring. One problem: you have no money. Websites cost money. Business cards cost money. Even bad ones.

KEVIN:

I've got some savings. Enough to get started.

ROB:

I've got nothing. My wife controls our accounts.

The energy shifts. This is complicated territory.

KEVIN:

When's the last time you talked to her?

ROB:

Two weeks ago. Five minutes. She asked how I was. I asked how she was. We ran out of things to say.

KEVIN:

I'm sorry.

ROB:

It's fine.

KEVIN:

It's not fine.

ROB *(after a pause)*:

No. It's not. I keep thinking she'll call and say she understands. That she sees what I was trying to do. But that's not how it works. She didn't marry Money Rain Rob. She married Safe Rob. And Safe Rob broke the deal.

KEVIN:

Maybe when she sees what you're building...

ROB:

Don't. Don't do the thing where you promise me she'll come around. You don't know that. I don't know that.

***KEVIN** nods. Shuts up.*

ROB:

What about you? You said your dad hasn't called in three years. Not even after forty million people watched your escapades.

***KEVIN'S** turn to go still.*

KEVIN:

Nope.

ROB:

That's why you did it, isn't it? The awards show. Not just for the audience. For him.

Long pause.

KEVIN:

I wanted to do something so big he'd have to see it. So undeniable he couldn't pretend I didn't exist. Forty million people watched. And he still didn't call.

ROB:

His loss.

KEVIN:

That's what people say. But it doesn't feel like his loss. It feels like mine.

Silence. The planning energy has drained. What's left is two men sitting with their wounds.

ROB:

My dad died three months before I did the money rain.

***KEVIN** looks at him.*

ROB:

Nobody knows that. I didn't tell anyone. Not even my wife. I went to the funeral, sat through it, went back to work.

KEVIN:

Rob...

ROB:

He thought real estate was selling lies to desperate people. Thought I'd sold out. Become everything he hated. Safe. Corporate. Boring. And he was right. I HAD become boring. And then he died. And I never got to prove him wrong. Never got to show him I could be interesting AND successful.

Beat.

ROB:

So I rented a plane. And from the time the money started falling to the time the cops showed up, I felt alive. Like I'd finally done something he might have respected.

KEVIN:

A twelve-million-dollar goodbye.

ROB:

A thirty-five-hundred-dollar goodbye that cost twelve million in damages. But yeah.

Almost a smile from both of them.

KEVIN:

You know what my acting teacher told me? After I bombed a scene in front of the whole class. Everyone said I should quit. And this teacher, he looks at me and says, "You remind me of Alec Guinness."

ROB:

Obi-Wan Kenobi?

KEVIN:

That's what I said. But the teacher goes, "No, no. Before Star Wars. One of the greatest actors who ever lived. And you know what HIS teacher told him? Go away. Go live life. Fail. Struggle. Experience the world. Then come back." So my teacher's trying to set me up with more classes, more coaching, more preparing. And I said, "No. I'm taking Guinness's teacher's advice." And I walked out.

ROB:

And started crashing things.

KEVIN:

And started crashing things. Because I figured if I couldn't get invited onto the stage, I'd take one.

Pause.

ROB:

We're both just guys who couldn't get invited. So we showed up anyway.

KEVIN:

And got arrested for it.

ROB:

And got arrested for it.

They sit with that. Then:

ROB:

That's the pitch.

KEVIN:

What?

ROB:

What you just said. What we both just said. That's the real pitch. Not the polished version. Not the tagline. THIS. Two guys who couldn't get invited so they showed up anyway. Who got knocked down and decided to build something from the floor. That's what people connect to. Not the clever branding. The truth.

***KEVIN** is looking at **ROB** like he's seeing him clearly for the first time.*

KEVIN:

You really are good at this.

ROB:

I'm good at seeing what's real. You're good at making people listen. That's why this works.

THE SAGE *(offstage, quietly)*:

The performer and the mirror. Each one shows the other what he cannot see alone.

KEVIN:

Sage dropping poetry on us.

THE CRITIC:

The Hallmark Channel wishes it had this much sentimentality.

KEVIN:

And there's Critic, right on cue.

CLICKS:

For real though, when you guys launch, I want to see it. I want to watch this thing grow. Send updates.

KEVIN:

How? You're in prison.

CLICKS:

Letters, man. Old school. Tell us everything. The wins, the losses. We're invested now.

CHALK:

I'm not invested.

RADAR:

Chalk, you've been listening to every word for twenty minutes.

CHALK:

I listen to everything. Doesn't mean I'm invested.

RADAR *(to **KEVIN** and **ROB**)*:

He's invested.

OFFICER MARTINEZ *walks by. Stops at the bars. Looks at the papers scattered everywhere.*

MARTINEZ:

This isn't a corporate office, gentlemen. It's a cell. Keep it clean.

KEVIN:

Yes, ma'am. But in our defense, we're building an empire.

MARTINEZ:

Build your empire on one bunk. The other one needs to be inspection-ready by morning.

She starts to walk away, then stops. Turns back.

MARTINEZ:

Richardson. Five weeks.

KEVIN:

Five weeks.

MARTINEZ:

Don't waste them.

She walks away. ***KEVIN*** *and* ***ROB*** *look at each other.*

ROB:

Five weeks. You're really leaving soon.

KEVIN:

Yeah.

ROB:

What happens when you walk out of here and realize this was all just… prison talk? Two guys with nothing to do making plans they'll never follow through on?

KEVIN:

That's not going to happen.

ROB:

How do you know?

KEVIN:

Because I've never had a partner before. I've had audiences. Followers. People who watched. But never someone who pushed back. Who told me my pitch was sloppy. Who made me better by being honest. I'm not walking away from that.

ROB:

You might feel differently when you're out there. When you've got options. When you're not stuck in a cell with me.

KEVIN:

I'm not stuck with you. I chose you. There's a difference.

That sits between them.

ROB:

Nobody's ever chosen me before. For anything that mattered.

KEVIN:

Well, get used to it. Because when you get out, I'm going to be standing there with LLC papers and a client list and a plan. And you're going to walk out those doors and we're going to build this thing for real.

ROB:

And if we fail?

KEVIN:

We already covered this. We fail together.

ROB:

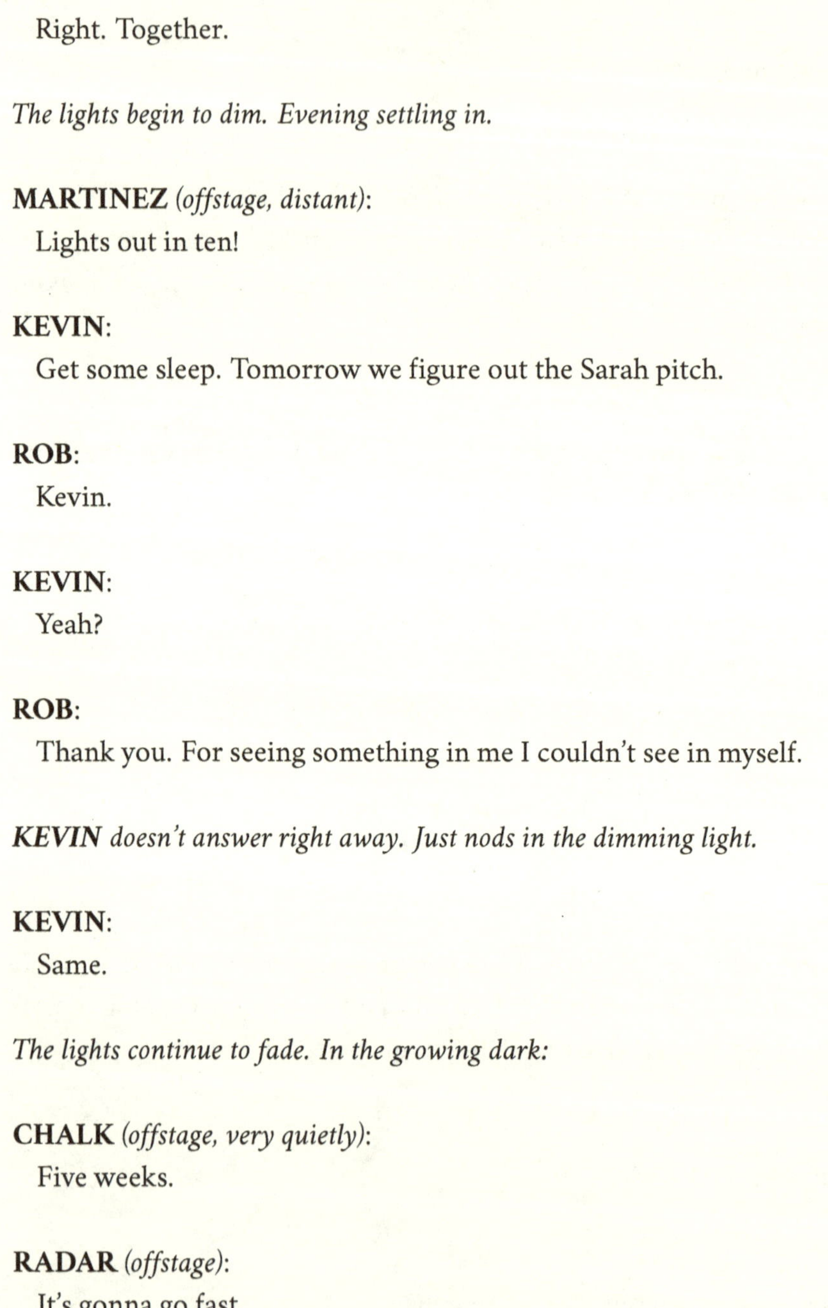

Right. Together.

The lights begin to dim. Evening settling in.

MARTINEZ *(offstage, distant)*:

Lights out in ten!

KEVIN:

Get some sleep. Tomorrow we figure out the Sarah pitch.

ROB:

Kevin.

KEVIN:

Yeah?

ROB:

Thank you. For seeing something in me I couldn't see in myself.

***KEVIN** doesn't answer right away. Just nods in the dimming light.*

KEVIN:

Same.

The lights continue to fade. In the growing dark:

CHALK *(offstage, very quietly)*:

Five weeks.

RADAR *(offstage)*:

It's gonna go fast.

CHALK:

It always does.

Complete darkness.

Blackout.

END SCENE 1

ACT TWO: SCENE TWO

SCENE 2: THE COST

*Late night. Two weeks later. The cell is dark except for a faint glow: the contraband **PHONE'S** screen illuminating **KEVIN'S** face from below. He's sitting on his bunk, staring at the phone. Has been for a while. **ROB** is on his bunk above, awake, watching the light shift on the ceiling.*

ROB:

You've been staring at that thing for an hour.

KEVIN:

I'm fine.

ROB:

You're not fine. You haven't made a joke in three hours. That's a personal record.

***KEVIN** doesn't laugh. Doesn't respond. **ROB** sits up.*

ROB:

Kevin. Talk to me.

*Long pause. **KEVIN** sets the phone down.*

KEVIN:

I keep watching it. The awards show. My seven minutes. And I'm trying to figure out who that guy is.

ROB:

That guy is you.

KEVIN:

Is he? Because in here, I'm the guy who DID that. It's my story. My credential. Every time I tell it, I know who I am. But out there? The guy in that video doesn't exist anymore. He existed for seven minutes on a stage he wasn't supposed to be on. And then they put him in a box.

***ROB** climbs down. Sits on **KEVIN'S** bunk next to him.*

ROB:

What's really going on?

KEVIN:

Three weeks. I get out in three weeks. And I don't know who I am without this place.

Beat.

KEVIN:

In here, I've got a role. I'm the comedian. The legend of Block C. I've got an audience that shows up every night because they can't leave. I've got you telling me when I'm full of shit. I've got structure. Out there? I'm a thirty-five-year-old ex-con whose own father won't speak to him, with a phone full of notes and a video that nobody's talking about anymore. That's not an identity. That's a résumé with a gap in it.

ROB:

You're not your video, Kevin.

KEVIN:

Then who am I? Because I've been the guy with the story for so long I don't know what's underneath it. Strip away the performance, strip away the awards show, strip away the guy whose dad watched forty million people pay attention to his son and still didn't pick up the phone. What's left? What am I without an audience?

ROB *is quiet for a moment. Then:*

ROB:

You remember what you told me? My first night here?

KEVIN:

I talked a lot that night. You'll have to be specific.

ROB:

You said optimism is a choice. That cynicism is what they want from us.

KEVIN:

Yeah. I say a lot of things.

ROB:

Did you mean it? Or was that just another performance?

That stings. ***KEVIN*** *looks at him.*

KEVIN:

I meant it.

ROB:

Then mean it now. When it's hard. When it's three in the morning and you don't recognize yourself. That's when it actually counts.

Beat.

ROB:

The video isn't your story, Kevin. It's the trailer. And the whole movie hasn't even started yet. You want to know who you are without an audience? You're the guy who saw a broken man walk into this cell and decided he was worth saving. You didn't do that for views. You didn't do that for a story. You did it because you actually give a shit about people. That's who you are without the video. That's who you are without the stage. And that guy is going to be fine out there.

KEVIN:

When did you get like this?

ROB:

Like what?

KEVIN:

Like the guy who pulls ME out of the hole. That's supposed to be my job.

ROB:

Yeah, well. You were busy having an identity crisis. Somebody had to step up.

The faintest smile from ***KEVIN****.*

KEVIN:

Did you just throw my own words back at me?

ROB:

Felt appropriate.

RADAR *(offstage, groggy)*:
Y'all know it's three in the morning, right?

KEVIN:
Sorry, Radar.

RADAR:
I'm not complaining. Just checking. You good, Kevin?

KEVIN:
Getting there.

RADAR:
Good. Because when you start doubting yourself, the whole tier feels it. You're our barometer, man. When you're up, we're up.

THE CRITIC *(offstage, muffled)*:
When you're up, we can't SLEEP. There's a difference.

KEVIN:
Night, Critic.

THE CRITIC:
It hasn't been night for hours. It's practically morning. Go to sleep.

***ROB** climbs back up to his bunk. **KEVIN** lies back. The **PHONE** stays dark this time. He doesn't pick it up.*

KEVIN:
Rob?

ROB:
Yeah?

KEVIN:

Thanks.

ROB:

That's what partners do.

Darkness. Silence. Time passes.

LIGHTS SHIFT*: morning. Bright, institutional fluorescence. A new day.* ***KEVIN*** *is at the bars, talking to the tier, energy restored. He's working through pitch ideas, using the tier as a test audience.* ***ROB*** *is on his bunk, reading a* ***LETTER****. His face changes as he reads: not devastation this time. Something more complicated.*

KEVIN *(to the tier)*:

...so the Sarah angle would be: Bulletproof Glass. We position her comeback as intentional. Not an apology tour. Not damage control. A RE-LAUNCH. She made a joke. They punished her for it. We help her make that the story: the comedian who refused to apologize for being funny.

CLICKS:

That's strong. But she needs new material to anchor it. You can't relaunch on the old joke. You need a new moment that redefines her.

KEVIN:

Exactly. So we produce a special. Short. Raw. Just her on a stage, saying everything she wasn't allowed to say. No network. No filter. We film it, release it independently, and let the audience decide.

CHALK:

Who's paying for the production?

KEVIN:

She is. Or a sponsor. Or we crowdfund it. The story of her comeback IS the marketing. People will pay to watch someone fight back.

CHALK:
Maybe. If she's brave enough.

KEVIN:
That's our job. Making people brave enough. Rob, what do you… Rob?

ROB *is still staring at the letter.* ***KEVIN*** *notices.*

KEVIN:
What is it?

ROB *folds the letter carefully. Sets it beside him. His movements are deliberate, controlled.*

ROB:
It's from my wife.

The tier goes quiet.

KEVIN:
And?

ROB:
She wants to try again.

KEVIN:
Rob, that's great…

ROB:
There's a condition.

Beat.

ROB:

Her brother-in-law runs a real estate firm. He's offered me a position. Licensed, salaried, benefits. Normal. She says if I take the job when I get out, if I commit to stability, to being the person she married, she'll be there. She'll try.

Silence.

KEVIN:

What about the company?

ROB:

She doesn't mention it. She doesn't know about it. I never told her.

KEVIN:

Why not?

ROB:

Because if I told her I was planning to start a viral marketing company with my cellmate, she would've stopped writing entirely.

KEVIN *can't argue with that.*

RADAR *(offstage, carefully)*:

Rob... that's your wife. That's your marriage.

CHALK:

Salaried position. Benefits. That's not nothing, Rob.

CLICKS *(offstage)*:

But that's also Safe Rob. That's the version of you that got you here in the first place.

THE CRITIC:

The version of him that got him here was RECKLESS Rob. Safe Rob had a wife, a career, and a house.

CLICKS:

Safe Rob was miserable enough to rent a plane and drop fake money over a city. That's not safety. That's a pressure cooker.

***KEVIN** hasn't spoken. He's watching **ROB**.*

KEVIN:

What do you want to do?

ROB:

I don't know.

KEVIN:

Yes you do.

ROB:

Don't tell me what I know.

KEVIN:

I'm not telling you. I'm asking. If there were no consequences, no guilt, no fear, no obligation, what would you choose?

ROB:

That's not how life works. There ARE consequences.

KEVIN:

I know. But you have to start with what you WANT before you figure out what you're willing to pay for it.

Long silence.

ROB:

I want both. I want her AND this. I want my wife back AND I want to build something that matters.

KEVIN:

Can you have both?

ROB:

Not according to this letter. According to this letter, I get one or the other. Safety or purpose. Her or us.

THE SAGE *(offstage)*:

I had a wife once. She gave me the same choice. I chose purpose. Built something I was proud of. And I've had twenty years in here to wonder if I was wrong.

ROB:

Thanks, Sage. That's incredibly unhelpful.

THE SAGE:

I wasn't trying to help. I was trying to make sure you know what you're holding before you set it down.

KEVIN:

Look. I'm not going to pretend I'm objective here. I want you to choose this. To choose US. But I'm also not going to sit here and tell you your wife doesn't matter. She matters. Your marriage matters. And if you need to take that job and be Safe Rob again, I'll understand.

ROB:

You'd understand?

KEVIN:

I'd hate it. But I'd understand. Because I know what it's like to want someone's approval so badly you'll reshape your entire life to get it. I did that for my dad for years. And it almost killed me.

Beat.

KEVIN:

But I'm not going to make this choice for you. This one's yours.

***ROB** picks up the letter again. Reads it. Folds it. Unfolds it. The whole tier is holding its breath.*

ROB:

When I was selling houses, I used to tell clients that every home is a bet. You're betting that this is the place where your life gets better. And sometimes you're right. And sometimes you're wrong. But the worst thing you can do is buy a house you don't actually want just because it's safe.

Pause.

ROB:

I spent ten years in a house I didn't actually want. A career I didn't actually want. Being a version of myself I didn't actually want. And yeah, it was safe. And yeah, my wife was there. And I loved her. I love her. Present tense. But she's not asking me to come home. She's asking me to come back to a life that made me so unhappy I rented a plane and committed a federal crime to escape it.

He sets the letter down. Final.

ROB:

I'm going to write her back. I'm going to tell her the truth: about the company, about what I'm building, about who I'm becoming. And if she wants to be part of THAT... she's welcome. I'm not going back to Safe Rob. That guy was dying long before he got arrested.

Silence on the tier. Then:

CHALK:

Damn.

CLICKS:

Rob.

RADAR:

You sure?

ROB:

No. But I'm done being sure. Being sure is how I ended up selling houses I didn't believe in to people I didn't care about. I'd rather be terrified and moving forward than comfortable and dead inside.

THE CRITIC:

That's either the bravest thing I've heard in this place or the stupidest.

ROB:

Probably both.

THE CRITIC:

...Fair enough.

***KEVIN** is looking at **ROB**. There's something in his expression: not pride exactly. Recognition. He's watching someone make the choice he made years ago. And he* *knows what it costs.*

KEVIN:

You know she might not write back.

ROB:

I know.

KEVIN:

You know this might be the end of your marriage.

ROB:

I know.

KEVIN:

And you're choosing this anyway.

ROB:

I'm choosing ME. For the first time. Whatever that costs.

Long beat. ***KEVIN*** *extends his hand.* ***ROB*** *looks at it.*

KEVIN:

Partners. For real this time. No take-backs.

ROB *takes his hand. They shake: firm, deliberate, eyes locked.*

ROB:

No take-backs.

They hold the handshake a moment longer than necessary. Then let go.

KEVIN:

Three weeks.

ROB:

Three weeks and you're out.

KEVIN:

And then I wait for you.

ROB:

And then you build. Don't wait. Build. Get the website up. Make the calls. Reach out to Sarah. I'll be here planning, writing, strategizing. We don't stop just because there's a wall between us.

KEVIN:

We'll write letters.

ROB:

Every week.

KEVIN:

Every week.

OFFICER MARTINEZ *appears at the bars. She's carrying her clipboard, doing her rounds. She stops, looks at the two of them, at the papers, at the energy in the cell.*

MARTINEZ:

You two look like you're up to something.

KEVIN:

Always, Officer Martinez.

MARTINEZ:

Richardson. Three weeks. You ready?

KEVIN:

Almost.

MARTINEZ *(looking at **ROB**)*:

And Wilson. You going to be alright when he's gone?

ROB:

Yeah. I've got work to do.

***MARTINEZ** studies him. Something in his voice is different from the broken man she escorted into this cell months ago. She notices.*

MARTINEZ:

Good. I've got money on both of you. Don't make me lose.

KEVIN:

You bet on us?

MARTINEZ:

Against three guards who said you'd never follow through. So this isn't just about your futures. This is about my two hundred dollars.

ROB:

We won't let you down, Officer Martinez.

MARTINEZ:

You better not. I already spent the winnings in my head.

The slightest smile from her. Then she's gone, footsteps receding down the tier.

ROB:

She bet on us.

KEVIN:

She bet on us.

The lights begin their slow fade. Evening again. The rhythm of the prison: reliable, predictable, almost comforting by now.

CLICKS *(offstage)*:

Three weeks, Kevin. You're almost out.

CHALK:

Time moves different in here. Three weeks can feel like three months. Or three minutes.

RADAR:

It's gonna feel like three minutes.

CHALK *(quietly)*:

Yeah. It is.

The lights continue to dim. ***KEVIN*** *on his bunk.* ***ROB*** *on his, the* ***LETTER*** *from his wife sitting folded on the shelf beside him. He doesn't look at it. He's looking forward now.*

ROB *(in the growing dark)*:

Kevin?

KEVIN:

Yeah?

ROB:

I'm scared.

KEVIN:

Me too.

ROB:

Good. Means it matters.

Complete darkness.

Blackout.

END SCENE 2

ACT TWO: SCENE THREE

SCENE 3: THE DEPARTURE

Morning. Bright, clean light: different from every other morning in this play. It feels like a beginning. ***KEVIN'S*** *side of the cell is packed up: a small box of possessions, a folder of papers. He's wearing street clothes: the ones he came in with, slightly ill-fitting after six months. He moves around the small space with restless energy, checking things he's already checked.* ***ROB*** *sits on the edge of his bunk, watching.*

KEVIN:

Toothbrush. Letters. Notes. Folder. Phone.

ROB:

Martinez is going to search you on the way out.

KEVIN:

Martinez is going to pretend not to notice. She's invested in our success. Literally. Two hundred dollars.

ROB:

You're betting your release on a guard's gambling habit.

KEVIN:

I'm betting on human nature. People protect what they've invested in.

He keeps packing. Repacking. Moving things from one side of the box to the other.

ROB:

You've packed that box three times.

KEVIN:

I know.

ROB:

You're stalling.

***KEVIN** stops. Looks at the box. Looks at the cell. Looks at **ROB**.*

KEVIN:

Yeah. I guess I am.

ROB:

You're going to be fine.

KEVIN:

What if I'm not? What if I get out there and freeze? What if I can't function? What if all of this... the plans, the pitches, the whole thing... only works inside these walls?

ROB:

Then you'll figure it out. That's what you do. That's what you've always done. You walk into places you don't belong and you figure it out.

*That lands. **KEVIN** almost smiles.*

KEVIN:

When did you become the motivational one?

ROB:

About five minutes ago. I'm faking it.

KEVIN:

Fake it till you make it.

ROB:

Exactly.

RADAR *(offstage)*:

Big day, Kevin.

KEVIN:

Big day, Radar.

CLICKS *(offstage)*:

You remember everything we talked about? The launch strategy? Social presence first, then the Sarah pitch?

KEVIN:

It's all in the folder. Every note. Every plan.

CLICKS:

Good. And get the website up within the first two weeks. You lose momentum if you wait longer than that.

KEVIN:

Two weeks. Got it.

CHALK *(offstage)*:

Kevin.

KEVIN:

Yeah, Chalk.

Pause.

CHALK:

I've been in here eleven years. I've watched a lot of guys walk out that door with big plans. Most of them, I never think about again. Couple of them, I wonder about. What happened. Whether they made it.

Beat.

CHALK:

You're the first one I'm going to worry about.

KEVIN:

Worry?

CHALK:

Not about you failing. About you succeeding and forgetting where you came from. Don't do that.

KEVIN:

I won't.

CHALK:

Write us. Tell us how it goes. The real version. Not the polished version. We'll know the difference.

KEVIN:

Every week. I promise.

THE SAGE *(offstage)*:

The path ahead is unmarked, Kevin. That is as it should be. A mapped road is merely someone else's journey.

KEVIN:

Thanks, Sage.

THE CRITIC *(offstage)*:

Try not to end up back in here.

KEVIN:

That's your sendoff? "Try not to come back"?

THE CRITIC:

What do you want, a Hallmark card? You're getting out of prison, not graduating.

KEVIN:

I'm going to miss you, Critic.

THE CRITIC:

I doubt that very much.

The ***JANGLE OF KEYS. OFFICER MARTINEZ*** *appears at the bars.*

MARTINEZ:

Richardson. Time.

Everything stops. This is it.

KEVIN:

Already?

MARTINEZ:

You've got five minutes. Say your goodbyes.

She steps back, giving them space. ***KEVIN*** *and* ***ROB*** *are left looking at each other. Neither knows how to start.*

KEVIN:

So.

ROB:

So.

Silence.

KEVIN:

This is the part where I'm supposed to say something profound and memorable. Sum up everything we've been through in one perfect sentence.

ROB:

And?

KEVIN:

I got nothing. I've been rehearsing this moment for a week and I've got nothing.

ROB:

The great performer, speechless.

KEVIN:

It's not a performance. That's the problem. I know how to perform. I don't know how to do… this.

Beat. ***ROB*** *stands.*

ROB:

Then don't perform. Just talk to me.

***KEVIN** looks at him.*

KEVIN:

When you walked in here, I thought you were going to be another quiet guy who did his time and left. I thought I'd tell you my story, you'd nod, and we'd spend the next however many months in polite silence. I didn't expect… this.

ROB:

Neither did I.

KEVIN:

You called me out. Nobody does that. Everybody laughs at my jokes or rolls their eyes, but nobody actually pushes back. You pushed back. And it pissed me off. And then it made me better.

ROB:

You saw something in me that I buried a long time ago. And you wouldn't let me keep it buried. Even when I wanted you to. Especially when I wanted you to.

They stand there. Close. Not performing for the tier. Not performing for each other. Just two men at the end of something and the beginning of something else.

ROB:

You promise you'll be there?

KEVIN:

I'll be there.

ROB:

With the LLC papers and the client list and the plan?

KEVIN *(small smile)*:

With the LLC papers and the client list and the plan.

ROB:

And a real meal. You owe me a real meal.

KEVIN:

First thing. Something that was never a powder.

Beat. ***ROB*** *extends his hand.* ***KEVIN*** *takes it. They shake: firm, steady, eyes locked. Then* ***KEVIN*** *pulls him into a hug. Brief. Real. They break apart.*

KEVIN:

The Viral Outlaws.

ROB:

The Viral Outlaws.

MARTINEZ:

Richardson. Now.

KEVIN *picks up his box. Walks to the bars.* ***MARTINEZ*** *opens the cell. He steps out. The door* ***CLOSES*** *behind him. He and* ***ROB*** *look at each other through the bars: the same bars* ***ROB*** *looked through on his first night.*

KEVIN:

Don't let the new cellmate have my bunk.

ROB:

Get out of here.

KEVIN *turns to go. Stops.*

KEVIN:

Hey Rob?

ROB:
Yeah?

KEVIN:
Your dad would've loved Rainmaker Rob.

ROB'S *face. He doesn't answer. Doesn't need to.* ***KEVIN*** *walks away with* ***MARTINEZ. FOOTSTEPS*** *receding. A distant* ***DOOR OPENS. CLOSES.*** *Another* ***DOOR. CLOSES.*** *Then silence.* ***ROB*** *stands at the bars, hands on the metal, listening until there's nothing left to hear. Then he turns and looks at the cell.* ***KEVIN'S*** *bunk is bare. The space feels different. Bigger. Emptier. He sits on* ***KEVIN'S*** *bunk. Runs his hand across the mattress.*

RADAR *(offstage, quietly)*:
You okay, Rob?

ROB:
Yeah.

RADAR:
You sure?

ROB:
No. But that's okay.

CLICKS *(offstage)*:
It's gonna be quiet without him.

CHALK *(offstage)*:
It's gonna be quiet without both of them going at it every night. My ears could use the break.

ROB:

You're going to miss it.

CHALK:

I didn't say that.

ROB:

You didn't have to.

Pause.

THE CRITIC *(offstage)*:

So what now? You going to mope for eight months?

ROB:

No. I'm going to work. Every day. I'm going to plan and write and prepare. So that when I walk out of here, we're ready.

THE CRITIC:

And what if he doesn't show up? What if he gets out there, gets distracted, moves on? It happens. People forget.

ROB:

He'll show up.

THE CRITIC:

How do you know?

ROB:

Because he chose me. And I chose him. And that's not nothing.

Beat.

THE CRITIC:
No. That's not nothing.

Quiet on the tier. The weight of that concession from the **CRITIC***. Then: FOOTSTEPS in the corridor. MARTINEZ passes on her way back from processing. She slows at the cell. Stops.*

MARTINEZ:
Wilson.

ROB:
Yes, ma'am.

MARTINEZ:
Eight months.

She walks away.

CLICKS:
Rob, when you're out there building this thing, you're going to need content. Real stories from real people. You know where to find a whole tier full of real stories, right?

ROB *(almost smiling)*:
I'll keep that in mind, Clicks.

CHALK:
And Rob.

ROB:
Yeah?

CHALK:

The letter. To your wife. Write it honest. Whatever happens, you'll know you told the truth. That's worth more than most people ever manage.

ROB:

Thanks, Chalk.

***ROB** stands. Moves to his bunk. Pulls out a sheet of paper and a commissary pen. Sits on **KEVIN'S** bunk: lower, closer to the ground, a different perspective. He starts to write. The **LIGHTS** begin a slow shift. Not the usual harsh fade to evening: something warmer. Time is passing, but it doesn't feel oppressive. It feels purposeful.*

ROB *(writing, speaking aloud)*:

Dear Kevin. Day one.

He pauses. Thinks.

ROB:

The cell feels bigger without you. Quieter. Chalk says his ears needed the break. He's lying.

CHALK *(offstage)*:

I'm right here, Rob. I can hear you.

ROB:

I know.

He keeps writing.

ROB:

I'm going to write the letter to my wife today. Tell her everything. The company. The plan. Who I'm becoming. I don't know if she'll write back. I don't know if I'll have a marriage when I get out of here. But I know I'll have a partner. And I know I'll have a purpose. And for the first time in my life, that feels like enough.

He stops writing. Looks up.

ROB:

I used to think mattering meant being safe. Being respectable. Having a career people could explain at dinner parties. Now I think mattering means being willing to fail at something you actually believe in. Even if nobody claps. Even if nobody's watching.

*The **LIGHTS** continue to shift. **ROB** is alone in a pool of warm light now. The prison around him is fading into shadow.*

ROB:

You told me once that this place was a crucible. That it would burn away everything that wasn't real and leave whatever was. I think you were right. I came in here a man who was afraid of being seen. I'm leaving as someone who's afraid of being invisible. That's progress. I think.

He folds the letter. Holds it.

THE SAGE *(offstage, very softly)*: And so the seed becomes the root. And the root becomes the tree. And the tree does not remember being afraid of the dark.

***ROB** looks toward the bars. The same bars he stared at on his first night, frozen, wanting to disappear. He's not frozen now.*

ROB:

Eight months. And then we change everything.

He sets the letter aside. Picks up the commissary notebook. Opens to a fresh page.

Writes at the top. He starts working. Planning. Building. The ***SCRATCH OF PEN ON PAPER:*** *steady, deliberate, alive. The light narrows. Just* **ROB.** *Just the notebook. Just the sound of someone becoming who they were always supposed to be.*

THE CRITIC *(offstage, barely above a whisper)*:
They might actually pull this off.

Blackout.

END SCENE 3

END ACT TWO

END OF PLAY

ABOUT THE AUTHOR

Eric M. Attio is a writer, storyteller, and real estate professional based in Vero Beach, Florida. His debut novel, Wine & Wisdom, was published in 2025 and tells the story of Ji Gong, a twelfth-century Chinese Buddhist monk whose irreverent humor and unconventional wisdom challenged the rigid institutions of his time. The novel received widespread praise from readers for its vivid storytelling and its exploration of the tension between authenticity and authority.

That same tension runs through The Viral Outlaws, his first work for the stage. Attio has long been fascinated by the role of comedy as a tool for survival and resistance: how laughter can disarm power, restore dignity, and forge unlikely connections between people who have every reason to give up. Kevin and Rob's story grew from a simple question: What happens when two men who broke the rules for attention discover that the real value was never the audience, but each other?

At twenty-one, Attio was cast in a Spanish-language soap opera as a menacing lawyer. He went home, learned his lines in Spanish, hated them, and rewrote the script. When he returned to the set, he never told his scene partner what he'd done. The cameras rolled. Instead of threatening the young woman as written, he opened with, "I still remember two shadows dancing on the sand…" and delivered a monologue that bore no resemblance to anything he'd been given. His scene partner didn't say a word because none of her lines applied anymore. When the director cut, he said, "Those weren't the lines we gave you." Attio said, "They were better, right?" The director agreed. Then he said, "You're not going to be the lawyer." Attio thought he'd lost the part, but the director continued, "We're moving you to romantic lead."

If that story sounds familiar, it should. A man throws out the safe version, improvises something dangerous and honest, and gets rewarded for the audacity. It is, in many ways, the story Attio keeps telling, from a 12th-century monk who turned Buddhist tradition on its head, to a comedian who crashed the Oscars and spoke the truth, to a real estate agent who rained money from the sky because being invisible was worse than being arrested.

Before turning to writing full-time, Attio built a career in sales and real estate, where he learned that the best transactions, like the best stories, are built on trust, timing, and the willingness to take a risk. He has also worked in college admissions counseling and telecommunications. His writing is informed by a deep interest in Buddhist philosophy, meditation, and the search for meaning in unexpected places.

Whether exploring a twelfth-century monastery in China or a prison cell in modern America, his work returns to the same conviction: that humor is not the opposite of seriousness; it is its highest expression.

The Viral Outlaws is his second published work.

For more information, visit:
www.ericmattio.com

www.ingramcontent.com/pod-product-compliance
Lightning Source LLC
LaVergne TN
LVHW051010080826
845145LV00009B/2546

* 9 7 8 1 9 6 9 4 5 3 0 4 5 *